ANDREA JAMES is a Yorta Yorta/Kurnai woman and graduate of the Victorian College of the Arts. She cut her teeth as the Artistic Director of Melbourne Workers' Theatre from 2001 to 2008 and is best known for her work writing and directing *Yanagai! Yanagai!* – a play about her father's people, the Yorta Yorta, and their struggle for land rights justice. The play premiered at Playbox in 2004 and was remounted in 2006 before enjoying an international tour to Wales and England. Relocating to Sydney, Andrea was the Aboriginal Arts Development Officer at Blacktown Arts Centre 2010-2012 and Aboriginal Producer at Carriageworks from 2012-2016 before embarking upon a freelance theatremaking and producing career. In 2012 she directed *Bully Beef Stew*, a play about Aboriginal manhood, at PACT Theatre, and co-wrote *Coranderrk: We Will Show the Country* with Giordano Nanni, which was produced by ILBIJERRI Theatre Company and the Minutes of Evidence Project at La Mama Courthouse Theatre and a reworked version staged at Belvoir in 2013. She was a recipient of the British Council's competitive Accelerate Program for Aboriginal Art Leaders in 2013 and was awarded the Arts NSW Aboriginal Arts Fellowship to write a one-woman play about Aboriginal tennis player, *Evonne Goolagong*. Andrea performed in her co-written play *Bright World* with Elise Hearst by Arthur Productions at Theatreworks in April 2015. She directed *Winyanboga Yurringa* (inspired by Hyllus Maris and Sonia Borg's *Women of the Sun*) which premiered at Carriageworks, Redfern, before touring to the Geelong Performing Arts Centre in August 2016.

Yanagai! Yanagai!

Andrea James

Currency Press,
Sydney

CURRENCY PLAYS

First published in 2003
by Currency Press Pty Ltd,
PO Box 2287, Strawberry Hills, NSW, 2012, Australia
enquiries@currency.com.au
www.currency.com.au
in association with Playbox Theatre, Melbourne
This revised edition first published in 2016.
Copyright: Introduction © Wayne Atkinson, 2016; *Yanagai! Yanagai!* © Andrea James, 2003, 2016.

COPYING FOR EDUCATIONAL PURPOSES

The Australian *Copyright Act 1968* (Act) allows a maximum of one chapter or 10% of this book, whichever is the greater, to be copied by any educational institution for its educational purposes provided that that educational institution (or the body that administers it) has given a remuneration notice to Copyright Agency Limited (CAL) under the Act.
For details of the CAL licence for educational institutions contact CAL, 11/66 Goulburn Street, Sydney, NSW, 2000; tel: within Australia 1 800 066 844 toll free; outside Australia 61 2 9394 7600; fax: 61 2 9394 7601; email: info@copyright.com.au

COPYING FOR OTHER PURPOSES

Except as permitted under the Act, for example a fair dealing for the purposes of study, research, criticism or review, no part of this book may be reproduced, stored in a retrieval system, or transmitted in any form or by any means without prior written permission. All enquiries should be made to the publisher at the address above.
Any performance or public reading of *Yanagai! Yanagai!* is forbidden unless a licence has been received from the author or the author's agent. The purchase of this book in no way gives the purchaser the right to perform the play in public, whether by means of a staged production or a reading. All applications for public performance should be addressed to the author care of Currency Press at the above address.

Cataloguing-in-publication data for this title is available from the National Library of Australia website: www.nla.gov.au

Typeset by Dean Nottle for Currency Press.
Cover design by Shireen Nolan for Currency Press.

Contents

Introduction
Wayne Atkinson   vii

Act One   1
Act Two   32

Currency Press acknowledges the Traditional Owners of the Country on which we live and work. We pay our respects to all Aboriginal and Torres Strait Islander Elders, past and present.

INTRODUCTION

Writing the introduction to this publication is an opportune time to reflect on the story that shaped the making of *Yanagai! Yanagai!* as a major Indigenous theatre production in 2003. The story of *Yanagai! Yanagai!* comes from a long history of land struggle that culminated in the *Yorta Yorta Native Title Claim* (1994–2002). This claim was an attempt to seek justice through the new land law that was passed after the historic Mabo decision in 1992. It is an epic drama that was acted out on Yorta Yorta soil through a decade of struggle with the Anglo legal system and one that had a major impact on the heart and soul of the Yorta Yorta Nation. Like our ancestors, whose spirits are now at peace in the ancestral lands, we carried the flag gallantly in the hope that justice would be delivered. This is the foundational point from which the narrative of *Yanagai! Yanagai!* rises and can be told.

As a claimant in the gruelling and divisive native title process, I am aware that this story remains firmly embedded in the memory bank of our people. The narrative builds on other stories of the land struggle that began at the outset of the European invasion and continues today. The oral testimony drawn from the Yorta Yorta case complements the rich repository of oral source materials that position the Yorta Yorta Nation as one of the many resilient and vibrant Indigenous communities in Australia. 'Always was and always will be Yorta Yorta land' is the voice of the Yorta Yorta struggle. Like the rivers that embody Yorta Yorta identity we will continue to assert rights that have been handed down since the land was created and endowed with the laws that flow to our people as inherent and sacred rights.

It is against this backdrop that the story of the Yorta Yorta word, 'yanagai yanagai', emerges from the ancestral lands. Similar words had already been asserted by traditional owners of Botany Bay in 1788. 'Warra warra' is the first word spoken to Captain Phillip and his crew, from where the path of invasion and destruction followed the rivers to Yorta Yorta country in the 1830s.

'Yanagai yanagai' was spoken loud and clear to the first intruders who entered Yorta Yorta traditional lands and waters. 'Yanagai yanagai' and 'warra warra''s literal translation simply means 'Go away', or at least, 'Go away until you observe the appropriate laws of entry and seek permission from the traditional owners who can then decide whether you should be given entry'. It is a word that is steeped in tradition and custom.

Whether it be customary law or the imported Anglo law, the rule of law as it stands must apply equally for trespassing on someone else's land. Yanagai yanagai is an assertion of sovereign rights and customary laws that regulated the ownership and control of land and access to resources. It is the original and oldest law of the land that demanded nothing less than full respect and recognition by the imported law.

Yanagai yanagai was asserted when the first white land-seeker, Edmund Curr, entered Yorta Yorta land and waters in the 1840s. Curr wanted land and resources to depasture stock on the rich alluvial plains that had been nurtured along the Dungala and Kiela River Flats (Murray and Goulburn Rivers). Nothing could be more invasive and destructive for the traditional owners than to witness such an alien culture and way of life forcing itself on the delicate balance that has been nurtured for over 60,000 years. Curr gained access to Yorta Yorta lands and waters through the generosity of a young Yorta Yorta tribesman who canoed him down the river to check out the potential of the river frontage and forest lands for pastoral settlement. It was on this journey down the river that he encountered a local clan group collecting fish from one of their fish trap systems, constructed across the mouth of the flood channels returning water from the forest.

Curr's journey into Yorta Yorta territory becomes one of the key scenes depicted in the play *Yanagai! Yanagai!* The play cleverly weaves together the narrative to expose the prime motives of Curr's entry into Yorta Yorta country and the conflict that takes place at one of the traditional fishing sites. Here Curr is confronted by the full force of yanagai yanagai. A young woman comes forward from the clan group and she plays a courageous role in keeping peace and calming the hostility between her elder and the invasive Curr. Her name is Underyarning and she is cast in the play to act out the power relations that were happening on-country and her courage in confronting the gun that Curr aimed at the tribal elder. Underyarning's courage and conciliatory nature made a big impression on Curr who noted that

'She was a good representative of her race in that particular'. Curr recorded this encounter in his *Recollections of Squatting* in 1883 and his observations and writings became the definitive evidence used by Justice Olney for determining native title in the Yorta Yorta case. This strange anomaly will be revisited shortly.

Encounters like these travelled quickly and beyond the bounds of old Dungala. Conflict and violence followed across the country with equal aggression as the frontier pushed into Indigenous land for the next century or more. Driven by the greed for land that the new penal colony offered, and the misguided belief that the country was unoccupied, or *terra nullius*, yanagai yanagai repeated itself across the linguistic diversity of the tribal lands. While it was an assertion of Indigenous sovereignty and ownership rights, the British Crown imposed its own sovereignty and assumed ownership of the land under the legal fiction of *terra nullius*. At the stroke of a pen Indigenous ownership of country, and 60,000 years of prior occupation and care for country, was struck down but not out. *Terra nullius* remained a barrier to achieving land justice for the next two centuries until finally removed by the 1992 Mabo decision. The playing field seemed set for an era of land justice to be delivered, only to find in the Yorta Yorta case that the legal fiction of *terra nullius* was replaced by the 'tide of history' euphemism. The tide had turned in our favour as we thought only to find that it was turned against us.

The 'tide of history' was used by the judge as a euphemism to cover over the underlying causative effects of colonisation and dispossession and to argue that it had washed away our connections with the land. The 'tide' concept was not a legal principle but an idea raised in Mabo that Justice Olney used in its absolute translation to deny land justice in the Yorta Yorta case. It was a cover-up job of massive proportions—still to be fully rectified.

The other impediment to Yorta Yorta justice was the way the materials of a white man were used to the exclusion of the substantive evidence presented by Yorta Yorta people. While Edmund Curr was one of the first intruders into Yorta Yorta country, his observations and published materials were given precedence over and above the majority of oral and documentary evidence presented by the Yorta Yorta in their case. The extent to which Curr was used as the definitive source of evidence in determining native title, and the way the 'tide of history' was construed to deny Yorta Yorta justice, still attracts wide criticism within the bounds of public, academic, and legal institutions throughout the world. In my own teachings of the Yorta Yorta case to thousands of students I have not found one who has been able to find sufficient grounds on which the take a pro-Olney view. This is supported by the general legal analysis of the case.

It was in this context that yanagai yanagai came back to revisit us as a metaphor for land injustice and survival.

After the failure of the Anglo legal system to deliver land justice, we needed to seek pathways that would allow us to tell our story to the Australian public and to the world in our own unique way. The power of the voice, spear of the pen, and collective organisation were political strategies nurtured by our leaders and carried forward from the Scholars Hut at the Old Maloga Mission (1974–1888) and Cummeragunja (1889–2016) to the cities and towns. They were the political strategies that fired the passion for justice and the struggle for land justice and racial equality. Cummera people were renowned for their fighting spirit and resilience, and their ability to bounce back from setbacks was all too familiar. The power of the voice and spear of the pen were the tools of empowerment that our people used to advance their cause. They are the foundations on which yanagai yanagai chose to tell our story through the medium of live theatre, music, art, education and community action.

During the course of the native title claim many of the younger generation sat and watched tentatively as the case was being heard. Some sat in the public hearings listening to the multitude of non-Indigenous landowners stepping up to the microphone asking questions about what was going to happen to their land, deaf to Yorta Yorta voices. (Private land could not be claimed, end of story.)

The mediation process was a travesty. It lacked direction and control of the way the media had misrepresented and often sensationalised the process. The cavalcade of the industry that emerged from the native title process was like a travelling circus in itself. So many chose to ride on the bandwagon of native title while the claimants sat patiently waiting in hope. Justice was certainly being seen to be done, but whether it could be delivered to the Yorta Yorta was the reality in the waiting.

Following the dismal outcome of the Yorta Yorta claim, and the way the law and the politics of the day combined with the media to pervert the course of justice, it was a time to reflect on our direction forward.

A talented and energetic Yorta Yorta playwright, Andrea James, witnessed these events as they unfolded, including the Olney judgment in 1998, which left us all dumbfounded when it took just nineteen seconds to deliver. Andrea was ready to take action and started the ball rolling. She wrote the script for *Yanagai! Yanagai!* and recruited a cast of talented Yorta Yorta and Indigenous artists. The task of writing and creating a play to depict the enormity of the story was a big call, but not beyond the passion for justice within and the combined talents and capability of the cast. The voice of yanagai yanagai, the denial of Yorta Yorta justice, and the desire to expose the way the native title process was conducted were the driving forces for the play. Live theatre was the way forward in telling our story to the world. Thus *Yanagai Yanagai* rose to the occasion.

The cast included some talented people of the calibre of Tony Briggs, who also produced the highly acclaimed play and film *The Sapphires*; Lou Bennett of the famous Tiddas and Sweet Cheeks bands; Bryan Andy, a very talented and versatile young man from Yorta Yorta country; Lisa Maza, daughter of one of the founders of Indigenous theatre in Australia, the late Bob Maza; and David Adamson of the Melbourne Workers Theatre, who had the unenviable task of playing the role of one of the intruders that copped the full brunt of yanagai yanagai, Edmund Curr. The cast and producer of *Yanagai! Yanagai!* are fine examples of the quality of talent that bonded together for the play's performance in Australia and overseas.

As we said at the end of the long and gruelling native title process, 'No tide of history will ever wash away what we assert is something that always was and always will be Yorta Yorta lands'—'We are here and we're here to stay' is the narrative that resonates through the power of yanagai yanagai.

The power of theatre as a medium for empowering the Indigenous voice is best indicated by the excellent and positive reviews the play continues to receive as 'Immersive and deeply affecting theatre—proof that, long after the song of justice falters, the strong voice of art carries on'.

As a tribute to the Yorta Yorta struggle for land justice it is important to conclude by saying yes, we did bounce back as our great leaders of the past would have expected. The Yorta Yorta Nation Corporation was successful in campaigning for land justice through the political process. In 2010 they achieved the declaration of the Barmah-Millewa National Parks and Joint Management Agreements for the future management of their ancestral lands. Their traditional ownership of the National Park is recognised and they are now in the process of negotiating for a hand-back lease-back of the land. A long struggle, but one that has brought positive outcomes for the Yorta Yorta Nation and the means by which greater self-determination can be achieved in the future.

Congratulations to all those who contributed to the making and performance of *Yanagai! Yanagai!* and to Andrea James and cast for all of the hard work that culminated in this publication. It was a great pleasure to be involved and to see the play achieve wide support and acclamation in Australia, New York and the UK, which certainly put our story and the Yorta Yorta Nation firmly on the world map.

Do enjoy, and thanks to the publishers for the opportunity to write the introduction which took me back to the scene of yanagai yanagai and bought me forward to the power of the Yorta Yorta and Indigenous voice in live theatre today.

Gulpa gaka anganya—gaka yawal ngulla yenbena Yorta Yorta woka. ('Welcome, friend—come walk with us the people on Yorta Yorta country.')

Wayne Atkinson
March 2016

Dr Wayne Atkinson is a Yorta Yorta elder and senior fellow at the University of Melbourne teaching Indigenous Studies. He has worked extensively in Indigenous affairs and was a principle claimant in the *Yorta Yorta Native Title Claim* (1994–2002).

Yanagai! Yanagai! was first produced by Playbox Theatre, in collaboration with Melbourne Workers Theatre, at The CUB Malthouse, Melbourne, on 10 September 2003, with the following cast:

CURR / QC	David Adamson
LYALL / DINGO 1 / UNCLE COLIN / LITTLE ALBERT / CHORUS	Bryan Andy
LITTLE MAY / DINGO 2 / LOLA / LESLEY / CHORUS	Lou Bennett
UNCLE ALBERT / CHORUS	Tony Briggs
MUNARRA / CHORUS	Lisa Maza

Director, Andrea James
Designer, Adrienne Chisholm
Lighting Designer, Phil Lethlean
Composers, Lou Bennett and The Crazy Baldheads
   (Tim Prince and Peter Lawler)
Sound Design, David Franzke
Audio/Visual, Michael Schoell

*In dedication to the lives of
Lynn Shadrach James (13.4.46–13.11.00)
Sofia (Zoshka) James (1.5.48–13.12.02)
and the new James clan—Nathan, Kobe and Dayna*

CHARACTERS

MUNARRA, a Yorta Yorta superhero thrown from The Dreaming to save her land; she wields a large digging stick.

DINGOES, two dingoes (ONE and TWO), Munarra's faithful companions; they are clumsy and hopeless, but have a good nose.

UNCLE, a 70-plus Yorta Yorta elder; he has come back to his river to die.

LYALL, a young Yorta Yorta man entrusted with the land justice dreams of an entire nation.

CURR, the ghost of Sir Edward Curr, a stubborn, sickly presence with a pale face.

TOMMY, a young traditional man, Curr's guide.

OLD MAN, an historical character, traditional, appearing in the re-enactment of Curr's arrival.

JUDGE, a courtroom character.

QC, a courtroom character.

HAROLD, an ancient murray cod.

COLIN, a Yorta Yorta man, Senior Aboriginal Sites Officer.

LESLEY, a Yorta Yorta man.

COW HERD, a herd of clunky wooden puppets; they shit on cue.

LITTLE ALBERT, Uncle as a little boy.

MAE, Uncle's little sister.

TELLERS, a chorus of four who play a variety of roles.

SETTING

Yanagai! Yanagai! is set in a mythical landscape on the banks of a mighty river. We call him Dhungula (the Murray River). This river is made before our very eyes. A sparkling celebration. The one constant. But somewhere in the distance she is crying. Touching this river, on either side, is the land. The landscape is expansive, like a plain dotted with ancient trees.

There are many trees floating in the space. They are as delicate and as wavering as the culture. They sway precariously when people pass. They are forever in danger.

Images and spirits sometimes appear in these trees. These trees are alive. Storytellers move behind and around them.

At the end of each story a tree is felled—like the pages from a book—each tree representing a memory, a person, a language, a culture.

There is a glorious high river bank which shows the midden timeline of centuries of existence. This is Uncle's camp. In bright blue neon, the word 'Maniga' [to fish] floats in the air—an ever presence.

In opposition to this camp is a line and an object which represents the ruins and ghosts of Curr's Homestead. An antique chair stands in colonial defiance. On this chair sits the ghost of Sir Edward Curr.

Large, wooden, clunky puppets with squeaky wheels represent a herd of cows. On cue, they raise their tails and shit. A giant cod puppet floats magically in the space, playing, swimming and teasing in the ancient watery playground below Uncle's camp.

Timezoned in The Dreaming, present and future, a clan of storytellers have banded together to remember a beautiful place they once knew. Together they tell stories that happened thousands of years ago. Some stories are told so that they may be remembered; others are told so that they may never happen again.

ACT ONE

SCENE ONE: STORYTELLERS' FANTASY

Four STORYTELLERS *stand in an empty grey space, their eyes closed. Finally, they speak.*

TELLER 1: We are here.
TELLER 2: We are here.
TELLER 3: We are here
TELLER 4: We are here.
TELLER 3: Expansive blue sky. Bright sun. Biami looking down on us.
TELLER 4: Clumps of Murray pine. Standing strong on the sand.
TELLER 2: Birds.
TELLER 3: Fish.
TELLER 4: Turtles.
TELLER 1: Circling eagles.
TELLER 3: Frogs.
TELLER 1: There are thousands of trees.
TELLER 3: As far as the eye can see.
TELLER 1: Redgum.
TELLER 4: Like blood.
ALL: [*together*] Our blood.
TELLER 2: The People.
TELLER 4: Forever.
TELLER 3: The trees hush and sing.
TELLER 1: They hold our spirits.
TELLER 2: The grass is soft beneath our feet. The earth is cool.
TELLER 1: The air is clean.
TELLER 3: And quiet.
ALL: [*together*] Sshhhh!
    Pause.
TELLER 3: The distant sound of the eagle.
TELLER 4: Crow.

TELLER 1: The corellas.
TELLER 2: Thousands of birdcalls. The flat grassy floor. Heavy air. Am I underwater?
TELLER 3: In this place there are thousands of reeds.
TELLER 1: Spears!
TELLER 4: The tallest in the world.
TELLER 2: Flood marks on the trees. At head height. The smell of water. Grainy sand crunching underfoot.
TELLER 1: And the river?
TELLER 2: Our beautiful river.
TELLER 4: Flowing. Ever on.
TELLER 2: Chocolatey brown. A few shades lighter than my grandfather's skin.
TELLER 3: The river is pure.
TELLER 4: We see right down.
TELLER 1: To the bottom.
TELLER 2: We see turtles!
TELLER 1: And fish.
TELLER 4: We call that one 'burnanga'.
TELLER 2: Murray cod.
TELLER 3: Big ones.
ALL: [*together*] That big!
TELLER 3: *True!*
TELLER 2: Heavy canoe cut from tree. Toe holes in the trunk. Thank you, tree. Poling down the river. Fire on the canoe. Catch 'em fish and eat 'em up.
TELLER 1: We dive into that river.
TELLER 2: Dhungala.
TELLER 3: Our life blood.
TELLER 1: We float.
TELLER 4: She carries us wherever we want to go.
TELLER 1: To the lake!
TELLER 3: The lake!
TELLER 2: Moira.
TELLER 4: Our beautiful lady!
TELLER 1: Full!
TELLER 3: Full and clear and bright.

ACT ONE

TELLER 4: Where the eagles fly!
TELLER 2: Ducks' wings hit the water. Bird chatter never stops.
TELLER 3: That one over there squawks like my sister.
TELLER 2: Wind high in the trees. A shiver in the reeds. Is there anyone in there?
ALL: [*together*] Sshhhh.
TELLER 4: Children laughing.
TELLER 1: Words echoing.
TELLER 3: So much to eat! Emu, kangaroo, yabbies, fish cooked in clay…
ALL: [*together*] We're full!
TELLER 3: [*recited under the dialogue which follows*] … possum, and turtles and swans and their eggs and ducks, snakes, goanna, lizard, big cod, mussels, duck dive for them, bush tomatoes, witchetty grubs, berries, yams. Good tucker.

The list is repeated until TELLER 2 *says, 'When we speak'.*

A soft rumbling of thunder.

TELLER 1: We can't move.
TELLER 4: Full of tucker!
TELLER 2: We have nothing to do.
TELLER 4: Just be here.
TELLER 1: And laugh and love.

TELLER 2 *begins to sing a song in language.*

TELLER 4: And tell stories.
TELLER 1: Thousands and thousands of stories.
TELLER 4: That fill us with knowing and comfort.
TELLER 1: And sometimes fear. When we speak—
TELLER 4: This beautiful language!
TELLER 1: Like honey.
TELLER 4: This language tastes good.
TELLER 1: It is ours!

They speak their language, enjoying every word.

Wardakau-nga nginiun yirriki-n. [*'A kangaroo scratched me.'*]
TELLER 4: Dhoma nynini yalka. [*'My dear child.'*]
TELLER 3: Yalka daya-n baka narrak. [*'The child is playing with the dog.'*]
TELLER 1: Ngini bana won-deya. [*'Here is a possum for you.'*]

TELLER 3: Galnya maaan winyarri-in. [*'The woman's face is pretty.'*]
TELLER 4: Yakarrumdja marri-bak. [*'Come on, let's bathe.'*]

They sense someone approaching to threaten their language.

TELLER 1: Wanin nyana? [*'Where are you from?'*]
TELLER 3: Wanin nyana? [*'Where are you from?'*]
TELLER 1: Ngina gaka daya minhetguda? [*'What do you come here for?'*]
TELLER 3: Woningenda pekka batima! [*'I'll spear you, you devil!'*]
TELLER 4: Wanin nyana? [*'Where are you from?'*]
ALL: [*together*] Yanagai! Yanagai!

TELLER 2*'s song is cut off. Pause.*

TELLER 1: No good.
TELLER 2: Almost gone.
TELLER 1: Taken.
TELLER 4: Gone!
TELLER 3: This beautiful place—
TELLER 2: Gone.
TELLER 1: Not there anymore.
ALL: [*together, quietly*] Only here.

They close their eyes.

TELLER 1: We are here.
ALL: [*together*] We are here.

♦ ♦ ♦ ♦ ♦

SCENE TWO: A RIVER IS MADE

Darkness. Distant thunder.

We hear a woman sobbing. It is MUNARRA. *She eventually appears in a dim and barren landscape. Covered in white ochre, her face streaked with tears, she drags a large, heavy digging stick behind her which makes a piercing and snake-like trail. At its completion* MUNARRA *bows her head and cries a river.*

Thunder and the sound of rain is heard. Heavy and then light. Sounds of sobbing and mourning seep out of the landscape. The rain stops and the trickle of a river is heard. Faint images of water, river and reflected light surround the space. The river is made.

ACT ONE

♦ ♦ ♦ ♦ ♦

SCENE THREE: GONE FISHIN'

Uncle's camp on the edge of the Murray River [Dhungala].
UNCLE *is wearing three jumpers, trousers and a hat. The Yorta Yorta word 'maniga' [to fish] is projected in neon in the sky. He is quietly fishing and at one with the land.* LYALL *enters. He hesitates and finally approaches* UNCLE.

LYALL: Uncle?

> *Silence.*

You probably don't know me.

> *Silence.*

I've been living in the city. [*Pause.*] Uncle?

> *Silence.*

They told me at the mish where to find you. [*Pause.*] Uncle, I've been—

UNCLE: Go away! I don't want to talk. I'm tired of talking. Talking all the time. I'm living here in this old whatsoname till I find my young time again. My whatsoname?... Dreaming! A man's come here for some peace and quiet. Nup, no good. Talking. Never done anyone any good. Never did me any bloody good. Don't you fullas know how to be quiet? Talk, talk, talk, talk, talk, talk. Bloody talking all the time…

> UNCLE *fishes in silence.*

LYALL: [*waiting uncomfortably*] Uncle, I was just…
UNCLE: You still here?!

> *Silence.*

LYALL: I'm Lyall. Lyall Jackson.

> *Silence.*

My grandfather was Garfield Jackson.

> *Silence.*

Did you know Garfield?

Silence.

They told me at the mish where to find you.

Silence.

My mum and dad are Lance and Prissy.

Silence.

My grandmother was a Campbell.

Silence.

You know that mob?
UNCLE: Yep.
LYALL: They're from Cummeragunja.

Silence.

LYALL *approaches.*

Uncle, I'm working on that land claim with those fullas in the city.

UNCLE *fishes in silence.* LYALL *waits uncomfortably.*

These fullas, they—
UNCLE: Yeah, I heard ya! [*Pause.*] They white?
LYALL: They're gonna help us get our land back.
UNCLE: This *is* our land. This is my tree, that's my river and there's a one-hundred-year-old Murray cod down there that's got my name on him. I don't need no whitefullas helping me out. I've been helped enough!

Silence.

LYALL *goes to leave.*

LYALL: Auntie Betty asked me to give these to you.

He puts a blanket and a plastic Coles bag of food next to UNCLE.

UNCLE: I don't want no supermarket food.
LYALL: I'll come around tomorrow, ay? I'm staying at the mish.
UNCLE: I won't be here. I'm going to the Bend. Fishin'.
LYALL: Okay, Uncle.
UNCLE: Sshhhh! [*He points to the fish.*] You're scaring the fish!
LYALL: Okay. It's been good talking to ya.
UNCLE: Sshhhh!

LYALL *exits.* UNCLE *fishes.*

ACT ONE

♦ ♦ ♦ ♦ ♦

SCENE FOUR: MUNARRA HAS LANDED

Darkness. Thunder.

MUNARRA *enters, walking by the river. She is homesick.*

MUNARRA: [*looking around*] Where the hell am I? [*More looking*] Where the bloody hell am I? [*Yelling up at the sky*] Why did you throw me down?! After all I've done for you!

Thunder.

She picks up her digging stick and swipes at the sky.

[*Yelling to the sky*] Ahhhhhhhhhhh! Why did you chuck me out?!

More thunder.

Get down here! Come on! I'm your wife! Come on! Ahhhhhhhh!

Thunder.

Two DINGOES *drop from the sky.*

Oh, great! And who are you?

DINGO 1: We's your faithful companions.

DINGO 2: We's your protectors.

MUNARRA: [*yelling to the sky*] Why me?!

DINGO 1: Ay! Biami, he's our creator.

DINGO 2: You wanna show him respect, girl!

MUNARRA: Yeah? Well, why did he chuck me out then? I'm his wife!

DINGO 2: It was with great sadness he cast you out.

DINGO 1: You've been chosen, ay?

MUNARRA: What for?

DINGO 1: A great honour has been bestowed upon you.

MUNARRA: Yeah, right.

DINGO 2: Out of all his wives, Biami chose you.

MUNARRA: He threw me out!

DINGO 1: Biami created you out of the fire, determination and spirit of one hundred generations of Yorta Yorta souls.

DINGO 2: Baparra-banarrak. [*'Long ago.'*]

DINGO 1: He saw your warrior instinct even when you were a girl.

DINGO 2: Even as a child, you roared!
DINGO 1: You're a representative.
DINGO 2: He chose you. You're thunder!
DINGO 1: You roll across the earth and you roar!

The DINGOES *howl.*

MUNARRA: What stinks around here?
DINGO 2: He's thrown you back onto the land so that you can save it.
MUNARRA: What is that smell?
DINGO 2: [*proudly*] This is our land.
MUNARRA: I've hurt my shoulder.
DINGO 2: Yorta Yorta land.
MUNARRA: Ooh. My neck!
DINGO 1: Our land.
MUNARRA: I sprained it!
DINGOES: *Your* land.
DINGO 2: Don't you remember?
MUNARRA: [*looking quickly*] Nup. Not here! It stinks!
DINGO 2: They've ruined it.
MUNARRA: Who?!
DINGO 1: That mob with no spirit.
DINGOES: Grrrrrrrrr!
MUNARRA: You talking in riddles! I'm getting out of here!

MUNARRA *attempts to make a hasty exit. The* DINGOES *catch her.*

DINGO 1: Munarra! Gathagana-ma! [*'Don't!'*]
DINGO 2: You're our only hope!
DINGO 1: Munarra! Grrrrrrr!
MUNARRA: Let go of me! I don't even know you.
DINGO 1: We's your faithful companions.
DINGO 2: We've been sent to protect you.
MUNARRA: Protect me? From what?
DINGO 1: Munarra, look around you.
MUNARRA: I've never been here before in my life!
DINGO 2: Look what they've done.
DINGO 1: The trees, the sandhills. This used to be a lake.
MUNARRA: I'm going back!

ACT ONE

She threatens to leave again but the DINGOES *catch her and force her to look.*

DINGO 1: No!
DINGO 2: You have to save this place!
DINGO 1: Munarra, look.
DINGO 2: Nhawul! [*'Look!'*]

They point to the apparition of EDWARD CURR *on the river. The* DINGOES *prepare to re-enact the story for* MUNARRA.

♦ ♦ ♦ ♦ ♦

SCENE FIVE: THE CURSE

The re-enactment of CURR*'s arrival.*

CURR *arrives in a canoe.* TOMMY *poles the canoe.* MUNARRA *watches.*

DINGO 2: [*motioning to* CURR *on the river*] Sir Edward Curr. He brought the curse. The curse of the sheep and the gun, with Tommy from the next door mob as his guide. He brought that whitefulla down in his boat, and sent her—
CURR: —merrily along with his rowing pole.
DINGO 2: Down our river.
CURR: Stately and hushed, old Tongala.
DINGO 2: Our beautiful river—
CURR: —flowed on through her trackless woods.
DINGO 2: Tommy is rowing Curr to our death! [*Shouting to* TOMMY] Tommy! You betrayed us! Stop! Go back!
CURR: The country on the right bank, he informs me, belong to the Moitheriban.
TOMMY: [*in unison with* CURR] Moitheriban.
CURR: And that on the left to his own tribe, the Wangatpan.
TOMMY: [*in unison with* CURR] Wangatpan.
CURR: The Yorta Yorta are a numerous tribe who have plenty of fish!
DINGO 2: And thousands of *spears*! Go away! You're not welcome here! Yanagai! Yanagai!
CURR: On rounding a point, a fishing party engaged at their work has come into view. Many of these people seemed surprised and displeased to

find a pale-faced stranger invading their vastness.

DINGO 2: [*brandishing her digging stick*] Yanagai! Yanagai!

CURR: The party was rather a defenceless one, consisting principally of women, old men, and children, the young men being out hunting, so that on seeing us, a general stampede took place for the shore.

DINGO 2: We ran for fear of our lives. 'White men! White men coming our way! White men who kill!' All around me the people are screaming and yelling. Water splashing. Bodies dripping. We ran behind the trees and bushes, trembling. [*Pause.*] And then our grandfather, 'Ngapa', charges forward to make war!

An OLD MAN *enters, furious and shaking his spear.*

OLD MAN: Yanagai! Yanagai!

DINGO 2: He's as wild as hell! 'Ngapa! No! Come back!' Yakarrumdja!

OLD MAN: Yanagai! Yanagai!

CURR: [*to* TOMMY] Speak to him! Speak to him! Tell him I mean him no harm.

TOMMY: Ghanu! Molwa gurtji nguni gathagana-ma! [*'Sit! Whiteman friend war don't!'*]

OLD MAN: [*shaking his spear, threatening and yelling at* CURR] Woningenda dhanu minhe? Ngina gaka daya minhetguda? [*'You want what? You come here what for?'*] Ngina beka muma molwa! Nyini Yorta Yorta wala maniga naika nyanuan. [*'You demon from grave! My mob water fish duck.'*] Nga dhupan nyunu wongingenda! Woningenda pekka! [*'I spit hate you! You ghost!'*] Woningenda pekka batima! [*'Devil to spear!'*]

MUNARRA: [*recognising the* OLD MAN] Ngapa!

DINGO 2: Yakarrumdja!

CURR: What does he say?!

TOMMY: He says, 'What you want? Why you here?' He says you demon from grave. The water, fish ducks belong his mob. He spits and hates you. You're pekka and he will spear you.

OLD MAN: [*charging with his spear*] Yanagai! Yanagai!

CURR: [*raising his gun*] Tell him to put down his weapon!

DINGO 2: We've heard what the whitefullas' guns can do. Bitja!

The words 'bitja' and 'fire' are projected around the space.

Ngapa! Yakarramdja!
OLD MAN: Yanagai! Yanagai!
CURR: Tell him!
DINGO 2: And then— [*Pause.*] The whole world stops. Everything stands still. Even the wind closes its mouth.

> *Pause.* MUNARRA *steps forward, finally remembering and realising her purpose on the land. She slowly moves herself between the* OLD MAN *and* CURR*'s gun.*

And then, the smallest and bravest girl walks out from behind the trees. We've heard that whitemen don't war with children. He wouldn't shoot a child, would he?
TOMMY: Gathagana-ma! [*'Don't!'*]
CURR: Curious to test the temper of the people, I whispered to Tommy to be silent, that I should not hurt her and prepared my gun for fire.

> *Pause.*

DINGO 2: He wouldn't shoot a child, would he?

> *Silence.*
>
> MUNARRA *regards* CURR *for a long time. The memories coming back.*

MUNARRA: I remember you!

> *She takes her grandfather by the hand. They turn their backs on* CURR *and she leads him safely back into the bush.*

[*Gently whispering to the* OLD MAN] Dhoma Nyini Ngapa. Gokwil! Dhoma Nyini Ngapa.

> *The threat, now passed,* TOMMY *and* CURR *are greatly relieved.*

TOMMY: Big one, stupid old man!
CURR: What name belong to young girl?
TOMMY: Andyarning.

> *They continue to sail down the river.* CURR*'s speech trails off into the distance as* MUNARRA *and the* DINGOES *speak.*

CURR: And again we float silently down our liquid road, between grand old gum trees, abundance of couch grass, and clumps of reeds, up which climbed convolvuli in vast luxuriance. Here and there crowds of ducks, and swans occasionally, take wing at our approach; the white crane, the blue crane, and the nankeen bird, with outstretched necks, look at us inquisitively from many a branch a hundred and fifty feet overhead. At times, too, wigilopka ['*the laughing jackass*'] salutes us from his leafy arbour…

MUNARRA: Curr!
DINGO 1: Grrrrrrr!
DINGO 2: Grrrrrrrrrrrr!
MUNARRA: Where is he going?
DINGO 1: He's going to make his fortune.
DINGO 2: He's gonna tell all the others and they'll come too.
DINGO 1: With their sheep.
DINGO 2: And their guns.
MUNARRA: Curr…
DINGO 1: You remember him?
MUNARRA: I remember him well.
DINGO 2: You were so little.
MUNARRA: Looking down the barrel of his gun is as clear as day.
DINGO 2: And his ghost still hangs on.
DINGO 1: Like a leech!
DINGO 1: Munarra, you gotta make him see!
DINGO 2: This place is sick and so is he.
MUNARRA: Curr. I wanna talk to him.

> MUNARRA *and the* DINGOES *watch the ghost of* CURR *float down the river and disappear.*
>
> *The lights fade.*

♦ ♦ ♦ ♦ ♦

SCENE SIX: SINGING THE COURTROOM

Three loud knocks sound out.

QC: This session has commenced. The hearing for the native title claim, Yorta Yorta Community and Others versus State of Victoria and Others.

> *The* TELLERS *enter. They whisper as if in a courtroom.*

ACT ONE

TELLER 1: We are here.
TELLER 4: We are here.
TELLER 3: We are here.
TELLER 4: We are here because we want freedom.
TELLER 3: Land!
TELLER 1: Justice!
ALL: [*together*] *Revenge!*
TELLER 1: Shiny floors.
TELLER 4: Foot-clomping corridors.
TELLER 3: Courtroom carpet.
TELLER 4: Sickly green.
TELLER 3: Wooden benches.
TELLER 1: Wooden panels.
TELLER 4: Shiny.
TELLER 3: Oh, so shiny.

Pause.

TELLER 1: Dust!
TELLER 3: In the cracks.
TELLER 4: On the edges.
TELLER 1: The hard-to-get-at places.
TELLER 3: On the wood panels. That cannot be reached.
TELLER 4: Wood from the bush.
TELLER 1: Hauled into the city to make this dock.
TELLER 3: Stenographers. Clerks.
TELLER 1: Black gowns.
TELLER 4: Wigs.
TELLER 3: Where's your war paint?
TELLER 4: This courtroom ritual is but a baby. Crying in a cot. Compared to our traditions.
TELLER 1: Judges that make you stand. And sit. Stand and sit. Stand and sit.
TELLER 3: This judge's bench.
TELLER 4: This hammer.
ALL: [*together*] Bang! Bang! Bang!

Pause.

TELLER 4: This isn't real.

TELLER 1: Not real life.
TELLER 3: Bored clerks.
TELLER 4: Powerful attorneys.
TELLER 1: Rolling in it.
TELLER 3: With their blank bodies.
TELLER 1: Unreadable faces.
TELLER 4: Dead-pan.
TELLER 1: Death.
TELLER 3: How do they sleep at night?
TELLER 4: We know how to wait.
TELLER 1: We are here.
TELLER 3: We are here.
TELLER 4: Because we want freedom.
TELLER 1: Land!
TELLER 4: Justice!
ALL: [*together*] Revenge!

> The words 'yapun ngutun wunun' [revenge] are projected onto the space.

♦ ♦ ♦ ♦ ♦

SCENE SEVEN: I AM YORTA YORTA!

Three loud knocks sound out.

QC: We call Mrs Lola Williams to the stand.

> LOLA *walks onto the stand.*

State your name.
LOLA: My name is Lola Margaret Williams.
QC: Do you swear to tell the truth, the whole truth and nothing but the truth?
LOLA: Yes. I do.
QC: Mrs Williams, what is your date of birth?
LOLA: I was born on the twenty-ninth of August 1934 on the Cummeragunja Aboriginal Mission.
QC: And who is your mother and father?
LOLA: Albert and Jessie Wallace.

ACT ONE

QC: And your father's parents?

LOLA: Well, ah, my grandfather was Albert Wallace. They called him 'Stubby' 'cause of his short legs. He married Jessie Charles and they had four boys and a girl. They lived on the mission. Two doors down from our house in that little street. That's right, and my great-grandmother was Lizzie.

QC: Thank you, Mrs Williams.

LOLA: We lived next to the Charleses and they painted their fence purple. That's right. And on the other side to us was the Jacksons and they had a little peach tree. And then there were all the families that were on the river. I can name all them too.

QC: Thank you, Lola.

LOLA: Yep. The Briggses and Alva and Gerald Morgan, the Coopers, Ada Atkinson and Henry, the Days and the Clements family. And we had a big school. There was Prissy Thorpe, Hartley, Selwyn, Glennis, Mavis, Johnnie, Jack was there. Ah… Larry, Bae, Thelma, Edna (she was keen on Artie), Gladys Briggs—she married a Jackson—little Albert and Mae Wallace—

QC: Thank you, Lola.

LOLA: —and Edward.

QC: Mrs Williams, can you tell us about your great-grandmother Lizzie?

LOLA: Oooh, yeah. She was real old. Tribal. She lived down the river. She had four teeth missing and wore this big possum-skin cloak all sewn up with the kangaroo sinew. I saw that. When I was a very little girl.

QC: Your great-grandmother Lizzie, does she have a surname?

LOLA: Oooh, no. Well, the old ones didn't have surnames in those days.

QC: Mrs Williams, do you call yourself Yorta Yorta?

LOLA: Of course! I was born and raised on the Cummeragunja Aboriginal Mission. Got married there.

QC: Is it not true that your great-grandmother was from Corranderk?

LOLA: Sorry?

QC: It is recorded on early missionary records that your great-grandmother Lizzie was from Corranderk.

LOLA: Ooh no, she's Yorta Yorta, I'm Yorta Yorta. We've always lived there.

QC: I'll present to you a copy of the Maloga Missionary list recorded as exhibit 18A.

LOLA: What's that?

The list is projected.

QC: Is the woman recorded as Lizzi on this list your great-grandmother?

LOLA: Yes, she is. She is my grandfather's mother.

QC: Can you verify for the court the recorded birth place written beside your great-grandmother Lizzie?

Pause.

LOLA: It says Corranderk.

QC: And do you know where the Corranderk Aboriginal Mission is situated?

LOLA: Yes, sir, I do.

QC: And can you tell us where?

LOLA: It's at Healesville.

QC: And is Healesville on Yorta Yorta land?

LOLA: No, that's Wurundjeri country.

QC: Thank you, Mrs Williams, you can stand down.

LOLA: We're Yorta Yorta! I was born and raised on the Cummeragunja Aboriginal Mission.

QC: Thank you, Mrs Williams.

LOLA: We're Yorta Yorta. Everyone knows that. I told you that!

♦ ♦ ♦ ♦ ♦ ♦

SCENE EIGHT: SINGING UP COUNTRY

At Uncle's camp.

UNCLE *is very hungry and still fishing. Occasionally he looks at the bag of supermarket food beside him. He reels in a line. The fish have stolen the bait. He sits and fishes, until he succumbs and takes out a can of tuna from the supermarket bag and considers it.*

UNCLE: See, old Harold! This is what happens to fish who aren't smart like you. [*He puts the can down beside his feet and picks up the fishing line.*] I'm gonna catch you today, Harold! You big, ugly Murray cod. It's ya old mate Galnya here. [*He waves a grub at Harold.*] Can you hear me? This was old Uncle Charcoal's spot. He was after you too, you old dinosaur fish!

ACT ONE 17

A large shadow moves in the water.

You've seen it all, haven't ya? You heard the songs travelling down the river. Upstream there where them big sandhills are. That's where the old river was, ay? Too much water coming up. Not enough feed so the old fullas they let it go. You saw 'em! Digging away at the bank with their bare hands. Their hands! They was engineers them fullas. Let the water go. Changed the course of this river forever. That was waaaay before I was born. I'm gonna go up there tomorra. Up past where the old fullas' camp used to be. That's where I seen them old fullas dance, up near where the big canoe tree is. That's sacred that tree. Don't you go telling anyone where it is, Harold! That's our secret, ay? Everyone told stories about you, when I was a little boy. You saw me, didn't ya? Up there at the lakes. When I first started hunting for you. I was seven year old.

The image of UNCLE *as a little boy appears, fishing in a little tin boat. He is in the exact same fishing pose* UNCLE *is in. He has been fishing for hours and has a hard look of determination on his face. Suddenly, he feels an enormous tug on the fishing line.*

LITTLE ALBERT: Wooo! I got something, I got something!

The line pulls ferociously, nearly pulling him into the water.

Woooo, watch out! I've got a fish, I've got a fish, I've got a fish! I've got ya. Ooooh, he's a big one. Hang on!

He struggles with the line, being careful not to tip his boat.

Hey, Dad! I got me a fish! A big one! I got him, I got him, I got him. He's a big fulla! I've got ya. Hang on, ya big fish!

He pulls the fish up to the surface and a giant cod's mouth appears.

Ooooooh! I got him, I got him, I got him. I got him. I got him.

At the other end of the boat a huge tail is splashing in the water.
LITTLE ALBERT *turns to see the tail.*

What's that? Oh, my God, it's the giant fish!

He drops the line in fright, grabs his paint tin lids and paddles his boat away at one hundred miles an hour.

I saw the big fish! I saw the big fish! I saw the big fish! I saw the big fish!

He paddles away until exhausted and then lays in the boat, slowly floating and looking up at the sky. UNCLE *holds out his arms as if floating too.*

I love it here. I'm gonna live here forever. Right here.
UNCLE: Yeah. Right here.

◆ ◆ ◆ ◆ ◆

SCENE NINE: UNCLE COLIN IN COURT

Three loud knocks and the words 'All rise' sound out. UNCLE COLIN *and the* QC *stand at a sacred site.*

QC: This out-of-court hearing will now commence. It is 11.23 a.m. and we are now standing [*looking at his compass*] due south-east at thirty-three kilometres from the Barmah Post Office. We call Colin Walker.

    COLIN *steps forward.*

Thank you. Colin, if I may call you Colin?
COLIN: Yep.
QC: Colin, you mentioned you are a senior site officer?
COLIN: Senior *Aboriginal* Sites Officer.
QC: And we are standing at what is known as an oven mound?
COLIN: That's correct.
QC: Right. And um, this *oven mound* is the subject of an investigation. And is the purpose of the investigation to determine whether it's a significant site or not?
COLIN: Yes, it would be, ah, looking to see.
QC: If this site is significant?
COLIN: It's sacred to us. This is an oven mound. It can be dated back to many, many thousands of years. People ate and camped here. We can tell by the food scraps and the old clay balls which was used to cook the food. This is a special place for us now. It's been handed down.
QC: Has the significance of this site been *determined* and *recorded?*
COLIN: We as Aboriginal people didn't have to go to colleges to get our degrees. Here's our university, [*pointing to the land around*] this is where we got our degrees from. And this here was handed down. Yep.

QC: Understand that, but um, the purpose of the investigation is to determine whether it's a significant site, is that right?
COLIN: Well, we *know* it is, because it's been handed down.
QC: And if it is decided that it is a significant site then it is *registered* and if it's registered it's then protected under the Aboriginal and Archaeological Relics Act. Is that correct?
COLIN: Yep.
QC: And if it is decided that it is *not* significant then it's *not* registered.
COLIN: This site has been here for thousands and thousands of years.
QC: But is this oven mound *registered* as a *significant site*?
COLIN: We know it is! My grandfather showed it to me when I was a kid.
QC: But is it *registered* under the Aboriginal and Relics Act?
COLIN: Look! Whether it's registered or not, this is a special place for us.
QC: Is it registered as a significant site under the Act?
COLIN: Everyone here knows what it is. Its importance!
QC: But is it registered under the Act?
COLIN: Not that I know of.
QC: Thank you, Colin. You can stand down now.

♦ ♦ ♦ ♦ ♦

SCENE TEN: A CAN OF FISH

Early morning at Uncle's camp. The sun is rising and bird calls ring out.

UNCLE *steps over the can of tuna, baits one of his lines and throws it in the river. As he looks into the river,* MAE's *spirit slowly appears. She is picking flowers on the distant shore.*

As LYALL *enters,* MAE's *image fades…*

Silence.

LYALL: I was just driving by. Thought I'd drop in. See how you're going. [*Pause.*] I've been driving around all day.

    Silence.

    Catching anything?

UNCLE: Nup!

    There is an awkward silence.

LYALL: You got a house somewhere around here?
UNCLE: This is where I live.
LYALL: It's quiet around here, ay? [*Pause.*] The land claim's going well. Nearly everyone's gone up to testify. Auntie Betty went up. She's seventy-two now. She told 'em everything she knew. She made us proud, ay? She even sang them a song.

'Bura Fera' is sung in the distance.

Right there in the court! The QC was asking her a question and next minute she stood up and sang right into that microphone. A Yorta Yorta song. Sang every verse right through to the end. There's only two songs left in language that we know of. [*Pause.*] Uncle, we wondered if you knew any songs you could tell the court about?

UNCLE *is silent.*

Auntie Betty told us you saw the old ones dance. Can you remember the songs? Any of the words. Even just one or two?

UNCLE *is silent.*

We went to the big midden near the junction yesterday. The whole court was there. You wanna see them with all their gear, traipsing through the bush with their microphones and all that. Bush court. They reckon those middens are like a timeline. Solid proof. Just like the scar tree.
UNCLE: [*suddenly interested*] What scar tree?
LYALL: They reckon there's a big canoe tree in the bush around here somewhere.
UNCLE: Who told you that?!
LYALL: Uncle Jim.
UNCLE: Well, he should know better!
LYALL: Do you reckon you could find it again?
UNCLE: I don't know what you're talking about!
LYALL: It's good evidence. For the claim. We thought you might know.
UNCLE: I've never heard of it.
LYALL: Will you take me there to see it? Just you and me.
UNCLE: I don't know where it is.
LYALL: That tree will be solid proof that we've been here forever.
UNCLE: Those trees are sacred!

ACT ONE

LYALL: Uncle, I swear on my grandmother's grave—
UNCLE: I told you! You don't go mucking around with that stuff!
LYALL: Uncle, you have to help us. You're the only eyewitness to stuff that nobody's ever seen. That's gotta stand up in court!
UNCLE: Don't come here talking all legal again. We've been fighting ever since whitefullas come here. And still nothing. This isn't the first claim we've made. Do you know how many claims we've made since whitefullas have been here? Huh? Eighteen! Eighteen bloody claims. You know what they did to our farm lots up at the mish? Mmm? Give us some land, then they take it away and give it to the farmers!
LYALL: That was back then! We've got native title now!
UNCLE: Nah, no good. You're not gonna get anywhere in those courts!
LYALL: It's our only hope!

> UNCLE *is silent.*

Will you take me to the tree?

> UNCLE *is silent.*

Uncle?

> *Silence.* UNCLE *fishes.* LYALL *waits.*

♦ ♦ ♦ ♦ ♦

SCENE ELEVEN: LANGUAGE IN THE COURTROOM—TAKE THAT!

Three loud knocks sound out.

QC: All rise! I call Lesley James to the stand.

> LESLEY *takes the stand.*

Please state your full name for the court.
LESLEY: [*tapping the microphone loudly*] Testing! Testing! One! Two! Three!
QC: Thank you, Mr James, please state your full name for the court.
LESLEY: Ahem! Lesley Shadrach James.
QC: Do you swear to tell the truth, the whole truth and nothing but the truth?
LESLEY: The truth?

QC: Yes, Mr James, do you swear—?
LESLEY: The truth is in the trees.
QC: Do you swear to—?
LESLEY: The truth is in the water, in the bush! That's where it is!
QC: Do you swear to tell the truth, the whole truth and nothing but the truth?
LESLEY: That's all I have left.
QC: Mr James, you must answer, clearly, 'I do'.
LESLEY: Bloody hell, I feel like I'm getting married—Alright, 'I do' as long as I can get a divorce later. Nah, only gammon. What was the question?
QC: Mr James, you must swear 'I do', clearly, before the testimony can begin.
LESLEY: Right.
QC: I will repeat the question.
LESLEY: [*blurting out*] I *do!* Sorry. You have to give me the question first though, ay?
QC: Mr James, do you swear to tell the truth, the whole truth and nothing but the truth?

    Pause.

LESLEY: I…

    Dramatic pause.

QC: Mr James?
LESLEY: … *do!* There you go. That was easy, ay? Ah, what was the question?
QC: Mr James!
LESLEY: Right. Carry on. Bloody hell.
QC: Mr James! This is a court of law. Unnecessary language will be classified as contempt of court.
LESLEY: Unnecessary language?
QC: You are required to answer all questions clearly and truthfully.
LESLEY: Unnecessary language.
QC: Thank you, Mr James, the court will be asking you a series of questions which will—
LESLEY: Manarraupna mutja!

    The words 'Thunder in your anus!' are projected behind LESLEY.

ACT ONE

QC: Excuse me?
LESLEY: Manarraupna mutja!
QC: I haven't asked you a question.
LESLEY: That's language. It means 'You are my friend'. Did you get that down for the records? That's M… A… N…
QC: Thank you, Mr James, we will refer to that term in due course. If I could just ask you one question?
LESLEY: Yep. Go on.
QC: Thank you. Mr James, can you please state—?
LESLEY: Woningenda dhanu minhe? Ngina gaka daya minhetguda? [*'You want what? You come here what for?'*]
QC: You must wait for the question, before you speak!
LESLEY: Ngina beka muma molwa! Nyini Yorta Yorta wala maniga naika nyanuan. Yanagai! Yanagai! [*'You demon from grave! My mob water fish duck belong us.'*]
QC: Mr James, you must answer me in English or this testimony will not stand in this court of law!

The QC *is banging his hammer. The English translations are projected around the space.*

LESLEY: Nga dhupan nyunu woningenda! Woningenda pekka! [*'I spit hate you! You ghost!'*]
QC: Order in the court!
LESLEY: Woningenda pekka batima! Woningenda pekka batima! [*'You devil to spear! You devil to spear!'*]
QC: Mr James! Order in the court!
LESLEY: Yorta Yorta woka deyawin! Ngunuk nga loatbaty! [*'Yorta Yorta land this one here! I am talking to you!'*] Lotjpa Yorta Yorta! [*'Speak Yorta Yorta!'*] Yanagai! Yanagai!
QC: Officers of the court, remove this gentleman from the stand! This court is adjourned!

The TELLERS *enter.*

TELLERS: [*together*] Always was, always will be Yorta Yorta land! Always was, always will be Yorta Yorta land! Always was, always will be Yorta Yorta land!

◆ ◆ ◆ ◆ ◆

SCENE TWELVE: WHICH WAY?

It is night. The full moon is drawing big, long shadows.

MUNARRA *enters, followed by the* DINGOES, *exhausted. They have been walking for hours and now find themselves surrounded by dead and dying trees.*

MUNARRA *enters first, charging ahead.*

DINGO 1: Munarra. Wait! Garraba! ['*Wait a little!*'] We're exhausted. We can't walk any longer.
MUNARRA: For once, will you stop ya whining!
DINGO 2: We can't keep walking like this.
MUNARRA: I'm on a mission!
DINGO 1: [*whining*] But we're tired!
DINGO 2: I'm hungry. Dungudja mulanwitj! ['*Hungry, very.*']
DINGO 1: We can't fight when we're starving.
DINGO 2: Please, Munarra. No more walking.
MUNARRA: Alright!

She stops suddenly. They bump into her.

Let's stop here for a minute.

They look around.

DINGO 1: Where are we?
DINGO 2: You reckon that this was the way to get to Curr's Homestead.
MUNARRA: [*sadly*] Everything's different. I don't recognise this place anymore. The landmarks have gone. The big tree? The meeting place?
DINGO 1: They stuffed it!
MUNARRA: Curr! Come on, let's find him!

She threatens to walk again.

DINGO 1: No! No more walking.
DINGO 2: Please let's rest.
DINGO 1: Nanyubak manu. ['*Let's sleep in the camp.*']
MUNARRA: Okay! We'll camp here for the night. Then we can keep looking in the morning.

She sets up her own bed for the night. The DINGOES *snuggle up close to her.*

Go away! Birra-ma! [*'Go!'*] You two sleep over there!

She shoos the DINGOES *off and they set up their own camp away from her. They all attempt to sleep. When they lay down, sounds come out of the bush. The* DINGOES *jump up startled.*

DINGO 1: What was that?
MUNARRA: Nothing! Sshhhh. Now sleep!

The DINGOES *settle back down again until they hear another sound.*

DINGO 2: I heard something!
MUNARRA: Sshhhh! Quiet!

She throws a stick at them. The DINGOES *cower and rest until another sound makes them jolt up.*

DINGO 1: Did you hear that?
DINGO 2: Where?!
DINGO 1: I heard something!
DINGOES 1 & 2: [*together*] Gukai!
MUNARRA: Aaaah! Come on then. Sleep over here. Nanyu-bak. [*'We will sleep.'*] Then we can get some rest!

The DINGOES *rush over to* MUNARRA*'s side and snuggle up to her, whimpering and fidgeting until they finally sleep.* MUNARRA *stays awake on high alert and slowly rises to investigate. We hear the gentle sound of droplets, together with bush and night sounds, intensifying, calling her. The* DINGOES *are restless in their sleep, but do not wake up.*

[*Whispering*] Dhoma nyinyi gutapka. [*'My dear baby.'*] Dhamala! [*'Grandfather!'*] Bakinal! [*'Cousin!'*] Wanhal yenbena? [*'Where are the people?'*] Wanhal yenbena? [*'Where are the people?'*] Winyanboga bapu! [*'Several woman, aunt!'*] Djiyaman gathagana. [*'Don't fear.'*] Yitja ngangwurra. [*'Heartache.'*] Dangalatj-djamitj. [*'Sorrow.'*] Dangalatj-djamitj. [*'Sorrow.'*]

MUNARRA *wakes the* DINGOES *and they quietly exit.*

◆ ◆ ◆ ◆ ◆

SCENE THIRTEEN: NO TRESPASSING

Uncle's camp.

UNCLE *sits by his fire and picks up the can of tuna. He's starving. He stares at the can for a long time until he gives up and opens it. He eats hungrily.* LYALL *enters with a brand new fishing rod, bucket and net.*

LYALL: Morning, Uncle. Thought I'd come by and do a spot of fishing.
UNCLE: [*hiding the can of tuna*] Oh, yeah?
LYALL: I can't go back to the city without a fish. Mum'll kill me.
UNCLE: [*eyeing off* LYALL'*s fishing gear suspiciously*] Do a bit of fishing, do ya?
LYALL: Not as much as I'd like to.
UNCLE: That's a pretty flash rod you got there, lad?
LYALL: Yeah, it's a Super Fine Aurora Trillium IM8 Pro Muskie rod.
UNCLE: I bet you catch a lot of flash fish with that flash rod?
LYALL: They told me at the shop that it's made from graphite. It's got these gold titanium guides, a reinforced fore and aft with a cork-grade handle.
UNCLE: Oh, yeah?
LYALL: You see, it's real lightweight.

He demonstrates.

UNCLE: [*checking out* LYALL'*s small net*] What, you got a net there too, ay lad?
LYALL: Ohh, yeah. Don't wanna let him get away.
UNCLE: You'll need a bigger net to catch the fish I'm after! In my day you needed a horse and cart to get your fish up onto the bank!
LYALL: True!
UNCLE: Well, lad, [*pointing to his handline*] this here is the Yorta Yorta 'Series Three'. All you need is a beer bottle, some line and a hook. It has to be a VB beer bottle though, ay? Oh, and don't forget, you need a carefully selected gum tree twig to balance ya line on.
LYALL: I don't do much fishing these days. It's hard for me to get out bush when I've got so much work on.

He is having trouble baiting his hook and pricks his finger.

UNCLE: What bait you using there, lad?
LYALL: Worms. Got 'em at the store.

ACT ONE

UNCLE: You won't do no good with worms. You've gotta use grubs. Here.

He hands LYALL *a tin of grubs.*

LYALL: Geez! I haven't seen one of these since my grandfather took me out fishing when I was a kid.

UNCLE: Who your grandfather?

LYALL: Garfield Jackson. Everyone called him Gundi.

UNCLE: Gundi! He was a good footballer your grandfather.

LYALL: Yeah.

UNCLE: Good shearer too.

LYALL: I miss him, ay?

UNCLE: He was a good man. Smart too. He helped the mob get a petition together. Sent it to the king. That must be where you get your brains from.

LYALL: I dunno. Sometimes I wonder what I'm doing in that court.

UNCLE: Hmph.

LYALL: I tell ya, some days I'd like to just sit on this river all day!

UNCLE *is silent.*

[*Looking into the river*] So, you reckon there's a one-hundred-year-old Murray cod down there, ay?

UNCLE: You ever seen a Murray cod, lad?

LYALL: Nah, never.

UNCLE: We call that one 'burnanga'. Murray cod. I've been after this big old fish for fifty years. Yep. Harold I call him.

LYALL: Harold?

UNCLE: Named him after me dad's old shearing boss. Harold bloody Whithers. I've got a bone to pick with him.

LYALL: Whithers?

UNCLE: Old Harold Whithers. Didn't like my father 'cause he was a better shearer than him.

LYALL: Me and Uncle Jim tried to get onto the Whithers' property the other day.

UNCLE: Did you?

LYALL: Over near Maloga. We were looking for that tree.

UNCLE: [*suspiciously*] What tree?

LYALL: You know, the big canoe tree out bush Uncle Jim told me about?

UNCLE: [*lying*] I've never seen it.
LYALL: When we went to check the place out the farmer wouldn't let us on there.
UNCLE: What? Who this fulla?!
LYALL: Whithers! When we got to the gate he came up in his four-wheel drive. He had a huge mongrel-looking dog in the back. Said we couldn't come onto the property.
UNCLE: Harold bloody Whithers. Come back to haunt me.
LYALL: His grandson. Said we had to have a permit! He locked that gate right then and there. Right in front of us! The gate had a sign on it: 'No trespassing. Trespassers will be prosecuted'. Then he drove off and left us in a cloud of dust.
UNCLE: No trespassing?!
LYALL: That's what it said.
UNCLE: Down near Maloga?
LYALL: Yep.

Silence. UNCLE *contemplates.*

UNCLE: Pack up ya gear, lad! We're going for a walk.

They exit.

♦ ♦ ♦ ♦ ♦

SCENE FOURTEEN: MUNARRA AND THE COW

Sunrise.

MUNARRA *and the* DINGOES *have been searching for* CURR *all night. She is having a child-like tantrum—sobbing and crying, big, long. pitiful wails.*

MUNARRA: I'm lost. I don't know this place anymore. [*Yelling up to Biami*] I can't save this place!

More pitiful wailing.

DINGO 2: Munarra, please. Don't give up. You're our only hope.

MUNARRA *continues to wail.*

DINGO 1: Don't despair.
DINGO 2: Stand tall.

MUNARRA: No! It's bloody hopeless. Where the bloody hell are we?

MUNARRA *looks around, trying to find their bearings.*

DINGO 1: I don't know.

DINGO 2: No good.

MUNARRA *wails even louder and starts to bang her legs, having a tantrum.*

DINGO 1: Munarra, please don't cry.

DINGO 2: Please stop.

MUNARRA: No! It's terrible!

DINGO 1: No, Munarra, no.

MUNARRA: The trees are gone.

DINGO 2: They'll grow back.

MUNARRA: The river's stuffed.

DINGO 1: You've got to have hope!

MUNARRA: What for? I haven't eaten for days! I wanna go home.

DINGO 2: You are home.

MUNARRA *wails even louder.*

DINGO 1: Munarra, don't despair. Sshhhh. Sshhhh now.

DINGO 2: Sshhhh.

DINGO 1: It's alright.

DINGO 2: Sshhhh now. Sshhhh.

DINGO 1: Sshhhh.

A cow wanders into their space and mooos.

MUNARRA: What the bloody hell is that?!

The DINGOES *tentatively guard* MUNARRA.

DINGO 1: It's okay, Munarra.

DINGO 2: We've been sent to protect you.

DINGO 1: Your faithful companions.

DINGOES 1 & 2: [*together*] Grrrrrrrrrrrrr!

MUNARRA: What is this animal?

The DINGOES *sniff.*

DINGO 1: Strange.

DINGO 2: Very.

MUNARRA: It's not from here.

> DINGO 2 *sneaks cautiously up to the cow's arse to sniff at it.*

DINGO 2: Look here! This fulla's got the biggest boobies I've ever seen!

> *He pokes at them and they wobble profusely.*

MUNARRA: Ayyy! Shame!

> *She waves her stick at* DINGO 2.

DINGO 1: Do you reckon this fella would make for good eating?
DINGO 2: Oooh, yeah.

> *The cow lifts its tail and does a loud, runny shit.*

ALL: [*together*] Paaaaaaaaaaaaaaaaaw!
MUNARRA: I reckon this one belongs to Curr. [*To the cow*] Take me to your leader!

> *The cow wanders off.* MUNARRA *and the* DINGOES *follow it.*

♦ ♦ ♦ ♦ ♦

SCENE FIFTEEN: STUMPED!

In the bush.

UNCLE *and* LYALL *are at a fence.* UNCLE *has some wire cutters.* LYALL *is on the lookout.* UNCLE *cuts the fence and we hear the wire release and reverberate into the distance.*

UNCLE: Harold bloody Withers. Come on, lad, it's over here. I remember now.
LYALL: How old do you reckon that tree is, Unc?
UNCLE: Oooooh, he's real proper old that one. Older than your great-great-grandfather!
LYALL: True!
UNCLE: Yep, this is the place, lad. I remember! This is where my dad and my uncles took me. You look over there! That tree, he's here somewhere.

> LYALL *and* UNCLE *look for the tree. Faintly the projections of old Yorta Yorta spirits are seen and heard in the trees.*

LYALL: Uncle, how will I know which one is the canoe tree?
UNCLE: Ooh, you'll know.
LYALL: How?

ACT ONE

UNCLE: He's a big old tree. Really tall, with a big canoe cut out up high.
LYALL: [*looking at a tree*] Nup, not here.
UNCLE: Keep looking.
LYALL: [*looking at a tree*] Nup, not this one.
UNCLE: Keep looking.
LYALL: [*looking at a tree*] Nope.
UNCLE: Ahhhhh. I can feel him now. He's singing to me.

Very faintly the wailing of the river is heard.

LYALL: [*looking at a tree*] Where, Uncle?
UNCLE: Come on, old fulla. Keep singing.
LYALL: Uncle?
UNCLE: Yep. He's here alright.
LYALL: Uncle?!
UNCLE: [*shouting*] I told you I could find this place!
LYALL: [*shouting now*] Uncle! Come here!
UNCLE: What you got there, lad? You found my tree!

He walks expectantly towards LYALL.

Let me see now!

LYALL *steps aside to reveal a tree stump and fresh sawdust on the earth.* UNCLE *and* LYALL *stare at it for a long time.*

Silence.

LYALL: Ever since Mabo they've been doing this stuff to our sacred sites! Burying them. Not telling anyone, when they see our bones. Sacred objects! They can't do this! Uncle?

UNCLE *remains staring at the tree. Silence.* LYALL *begins to walk away.*

UNCLE: Hey, lad!
LYALL: I'm sorry, Uncle.
UNCLE: You going to that court tomorrow?
LYALL: Yep.
UNCLE: Pick me up. Early. When the sun comes up. I'll be waiting for you.

END OF ACT ONE

ACT TWO

SCENE SIXTEEN: WE KNOW HOW TO WAIT

The STORYTELLERS *are in a courtroom. Images of ancestors are projected into the trees. They wait. Silence.*

TELLER 1: We are here.
TELLER 2: We are here.
TELLER 4: We're waiting.
TELLER 2: Waiting!
TELLER 3: Waiting!
TELLER 4: Waiting!
TELLER 3: For the judge.
TELLER 4: He's late.
TELLER 2: There's nothing *we* can do about it.
TELLER 4: Silence.
TELLER 3: Deathly silence.
TELLER 4: How much longer do we have to wait?
TELLER 2: For those men to make their decision.

An ancestor's image fades from a tree.

TELLER 1: Another death. Stories gone.
TELLER 3: How much longer do we have to wait?!
TELLER 4: What are they doing in there?
TELLER 2: Behind that door.
TELLERS 2, 3 & 4: [*together*] Come on!
TELLER 2: Don't worry about us.
TELLER 4: We know how to wait.
TELLER 3: Months, years, a decade.
TELLER 4: Waiting since 1881!
TELLER 2: And the men in the chambers mumble.
TELLER 4: Their tummies rumble.
TELLER 2: 'Let's do lunch!'
TELLER 4: We're waiting.

ACT TWO 33

TELLER 3: For our justice.
TELLER 1: Another death.
TELLER 3: Stories gone.
TELLER 2: Is today the day for justice?
TELLERS 2, 3 & 4: [*together*] Waiting! Waiting! Waiting!
TELLER 3: Three knocks on the door.
TELLER 2: 'All rise.'
TELLER 4: Stand.
TELLER 3: Bow to the judge.
TELLER 1: Another death. Stories gone.
TELLER 4: Is today the day for justice?
TELLER 3: The stenographer!
TELLER 4: Bored shitless.
TELLER 3: The clerk!
TELLER 4: Looks like he's done something wrong.
TELLER 2: Is today the day for justice?
TELLER 1: Another death. Stories gone.
ALL: [*together*] Give us our land!

Three knocks of the hammer.

QC: This hearing is to be adjourned until a later date.
TELLER 1: All rise!
TELLER 2: All rise!
TELLER 3: All rise!
TELLER 1, 2 & 3: [*together, slower*] All... rise!

The TELLERS *slowly rise up. Another ancestor's image fades.*

♦ ♦ ♦ ♦ ♦

SCENE SEVENTEEN: OUR PROTECTOR, THE RIVER

Early morning at Uncle's camp.

UNCLE *gets out his best shirt and puts it on. He kneels down by the river and washes his face. As he does this,* LITTLE ALBERT *and his sister* MAE *come floating by. He watches them as they dive into the water, laughing.*

LITTLE ALBERT: Come on, Mae! Swim, swim!
MAE: I'm coming!

LITTLE ALBERT: I'll beat you to the other side.
MAE: [*dog paddling and trying to catch up*] Okay!
LITTLE ALBERT: Come on, Mae, follow me!
MAE: Yeah, alright!
LITTLE ALBERT: Faster!
MAE: I'm coming!
LITTLE ALBERT: This is fun! You can do it!
MAE: Yes, Albert.
LITTLE ALBERT: Just like me. Swim like me. Watch.
MAE: Okay.
LITTLE ALBERT: Follow me.
MAE: I'm right behind you.
LITTLE ALBERT: When we get over to the other side let's play mudsticks. That's fun, ay Mae?
MAE: Yes, Albert!
LITTLE ALBERT: Come on! Faster!
MAE: I'm swimming as fast as I can!
LITTLE ALBERT: See those flowers on the bank, we'll pick them for Mum. Those little yellow ones.
MAE: Wait!
LITTLE ALBERT: Remember when you caught that little lizard and we took him home and you named him Mister?
MAE: Yeah.
LITTLE ALBERT: Keep going.
MAE: Albert! Wait!
LITTLE ALBERT: Just follow me!
MAE: It's too far away.
LITTLE ALBERT: No, Mae. It's just there. You can do it.
MAE: No!

   She stops and treads water.

LITTLE ALBERT: Mae! What are you doing?
MAE: I can't do it. I'm going back.
LITTLE ALBERT: No, Mae! You can't! Come with me.
MAE: Ooh, Albert! Too far.
LITTLE ALBERT: Remember what Mum said?
MAE: Yes!

LITTLE ALBERT: If you see the black car, jump in and swim to the other side.
MAE: I know!
LITTLE ALBERT: Come on then, Mae! You can do it!
MAE: Alright, wait for me.
LITTLE ALBERT: Good girl. Come on, you can do it! Swim! Follow me!
MAE: Albert! It's moving me away.
LITTLE ALBERT: Keep swimming! Keep swimming!
MAE: It's too far!
LITTLE ALBERT: Just a little further to go.
MAE: Albert!
LITTLE ALBERT: You're nearly there.

    UNCLE *shouts out to* MAE *too.*

MAE: Nearly there!
LITTLE ALBERT: Swim, Mae!

    UNCLE *shouts to* MAE *too.*

We're nearly there. Look, Mae, I can touch the bottom. See! We made it! We beat 'em!

    He turns around to look for MAE *but realises she is not there.* UNCLE *on the shore yells too.*

UNCLE: Mae?! Mae?!
LITTLE ALBERT & UNCLE: [*together*] Mae!

    The image of LITTLE ALBERT *floats downriver.* UNCLE *washes his face.*

◆ ◆ ◆ ◆ ◆

SCENE EIGHTEEN: ON THE HUNT

MUNARRA *enters, cautiously. Searching. Hunting. She whistles to the* DINGOES *and they enter. The* DINGOES *catch a scent and are sniffing madly.*

MUNARRA: What is it?
DINGO 1: Oooh, a smell.
DINGO 2: Ditjumurra! [*'Stink!'*]

MUNARRA: What kind of smell?
DINGO 2: No good.
DINGO 1: Like maggots.
MUNARRA: What you got there?

The DINGOES' *sniffing intensifies.*

DINGO 1: Oooh, bloody hell!
DINGO 2: A rotting carcass.
DINGO 1: Stinking flesh.
DINGO 2: Putrid!
DINGO 1: Rotten!
DINGO 2: A dead thing.

The cow puppet has entered and moos loudly. A light rises on CURR's *ghostly homestead.* CURR's *ghost is clinging onto an ornate chair in the ruins of his sitting room. He stares straight ahead, oblivious to the presence of* MUNARRA *and the* DINGOES. *A rusty bell and ornate tea set stand beside him. His gun leans against the chair.*

MUNARRA: There he is.

Silence.

The DINGOES *and* MUNARRA *regard* CURR *for a long time before they slowly approach and stand in front of him. He stares right through them.*

Hello, Curr.
DINGO 1: It's us.
DINGO 2: We found you.

CURR *is unaware.*

MUNARRA: We are here.
DINGO 2: Curr?
DINGO 1: We are here.

They circle him as they speak.

MUNARRA: We travelled a long way to find you.
DINGO 2: A long, long way.
DINGO 1: Curr.
MUNARRA: Curr?

ACT TWO

DINGO 2: Curr? [*Pause.*] Is he dead?
DINGO 1: [*yelling*] How ya goin', bruz?
MUNARRA: [*waving a hand in front of* CURR's *eyes*] Yoo-hoo?
DINGOES 1 & 2: [*together*] Grrrrrr!
DINGO 2: Does he see us?
MUNARRA: No... Yurrungurra. [*'Blind.'*] That's the problem.
DINGO 1: He doesn't see?
MUNARRA: He sees.
DINGO 2: But, does he see us?
MUNARRA: He sees what he wants to see.

    CURR *ignores them.*

DINGOES 1 & 2: [*together*] Grrrrrrr!

    CURR *leans forward and rings the rusty bell.*

MUNARRA: Sshhhh! Wait!

    MUNARRA *and the* DINGOES *take position and watch* CURR. CURR *mutters to himself.*

DINGO 1: [*whispering*] Who is he talking to?
MUNARRA: [*whispering*] Himself.
DINGO 2: [*whispering*] He's mad.
MUNARRA: [*whispering*] Yep. They're all mad.
DINGO 1: Madder than hell.
DINGO 2: Grrrrrr!
DINGO 1: Let's rip him apart!
DINGO 2: Into tiny pieces.
DINGO 1: Tear his guts out!
DINGO 2: Chew his bones.
DINGO 1: He'll make a good feed.
DINGOES 1 & 2: [*together*] Grrrrrrrrrrrrrrr!

    CURR *leans forward and rings his bell.*

MUNARRA: [*stopping them*] Sshhhh! Wait! Go back!

    MUNARRA *motions to* DINGO 2 *to go to* CURR.

CURR: Oh, there you are! I'd wondered where you got to. Five o'clock is tea time.

    MUNARRA *motions to* DINGO 2 *to pour* CURR *his tea.*

Not five past five. No no no. Five… o'… clock.

> DINGO 2 *hands him his teacup.*

We also have tea at eleven o'clock and tea at two in the afternoon. [*He sips his tea.*] Sugar?!

> DINGO 2 *works out how to put sugar in his tea, stirs it and hands the cup back to him.*

That's better. Thank you.

> DINGO 2 *joins* MUNARRA *and* DINGO 1. *They watch* CURR *finish his tea. When he is finished* CURR *rings the bell once more. This time,* MUNARRA *moves to* CURR's *teapot and slowly and deliberately pours a cup of tea, sugars it twice and pours in the milk. She places the cup delicately in her own hands and begins to drink.*

Excuse me?

> *Pause. They look at each other for some time.*

MUNARRA: Do you remember me?
CURR: I've never seen you before.
MUNARRA: I remember you.
CURR: Where is my tea?!
MUNARRA: There's nobody here.
CURR: It's tea time!
MUNARRA: Terra!

> *She sips her tea.*

CURR: Serve me my tea!
MUNARRA: Nullius!

> *She sips her tea.*

CURR: Tea!

> *Silence. She sips her tea.*

MUNARRA: It's been a long time.
CURR: Sorry?
MUNARRA: Since we last met.
CURR: I've never seen you before.
MUNARRA: Really? [*She sips her tea.*] And now I am your guest!
CURR: My what?

ACT TWO

MUNARRA: Your guest... of honour.
CURR: My guest?
MUNARRA: Yes.
CURR: An honourable guest?
MUNARRA: Indeed.
CURR: Oh... I see... Welcome!
MUNARRA: Thank you.
CURR: Welcome to my house.
MUNARRA: Most kind of you.
CURR: My homestead. Did you see the luscious crop on your way in? I grew that crop.
MUNARRA: I saw nothing. I saw dust and sand and cracks in the earth.
CURR: Come, please take a seat. Rest up a bit. You look like you've been walking for miles. Would you like to join me in a game of pool? A stroll in the garden perhaps?
MUNARRA: I've got prickles in my feet from your dead garden. See?
CURR: You're bleeding!
MUNARRA: It's the blood of my people, Mr Curr.
CURR: Would you like some cake? I have some excellent fruit from my orchard. Peaches. I could have them picked for you.
MUNARRA: Do you remember us?
CURR: I have some wonderful music I could play on my gramophone. Shall I play some for you?
MUNARRA: The people?
CURR: Game of tennis?
MUNARRA: We were on the riverbank.
CURR: Backgammon?
MUNARRA: And we're still here.
CURR: I have written my recollections down. You can read them if you like. They have been published into two editions.
MUNARRA: No... thank you.
CURR: Oh, look! There is my wife. Planting roses.
MUNARRA: Give up, Curr.
CURR: The sprinkler, dropping water all around.
MUNARRA: Let go!
CURR: Such lovely weather.

> *Pause.* MUNARRA *noisily finishes her tea and then places the cup inside her dilly bag.*

Excuse me, madam! That teacup is mine.
MUNARRA: What's yours is mine.
CURR: I must ask you for its return.
MUNARRA: Do you remember us?
CURR: I'm afraid I must ask you to leave!
MUNARRA: The people?
CURR: Get out!
MUNARRA: On the riverbank.
CURR: This is trespass!
MUNARRA: We're still here.
CURR: Get out!
MUNARRA: Don't you remember us?
CURR: Leave!
MUNARRA: I remember you.
CURR: I shall have you removed!
MUNARRA: We are here!
CURR: Get out! Get out!

> *He points the gun at them. Pause.*

MUNARRA: We are here.

> *They exit, leaving* CURR *on his own.* CURR *sits, clinging to his chair tightly. Silence. He rings the bell. Nobody comes. The lights fade.*

♦ ♦ ♦ ♦ ♦

SCENE NINETEEN: UNCLE IN COURT

The courtroom. Three loud knocks sound out.

QC: We call Mr Albert Reginald Wallace to the stand.

> UNCLE *moves to the stand.*

Mr Wallace, do you swear to tell the truth, the whole truth and nothing but the truth?
UNCLE: I most certainly do. I swear on my mother's grave.

ACT TWO

QC: Can you state your full name for the court?
UNCLE: I call myself Galnya.
QC: Mr Wallace, you must state your *birth* name for the court.
UNCLE: Albert Reginald Wallace.
QC: Mr Wallace, please state for the court your birth date and place.
UNCLE: I was born on the banks of the Murray River. January. Not sure which day. Around 1920. My grandmother delivered me in an old tin shed and I have not moved three ks west or three ks south from that place.
QC: Thank you, Mr Wallace.
UNCLE: [*under his breath*] Galnya!
QC: Now, Mr Wallace, we're just going to ask you, for the court records, a few questions about what you know.
UNCLE: I've got important things to say.
QC: Good. Can you please state, for the court, your mother's name?
UNCLE: Priscilla. Priscilla Louise Wallace.
QC: Thank you, Mr Wallace. Can you please state the name of your father?
UNCLE: My father taught me how to fish using an old canoe and spear. You ever seen that?
QC: Your father's name?
UNCLE: He'd get a long, skinny reed and tie it in a knot and put it down the grub hole, tease him until he bites then whip him up. He showed me that.
QC: Your father's name—?
UNCLE: He showed me where the fish trap is. At the cutting. If you head upstream from there that's where I saw the old canoe tree. A farmer chopped it down! It was a thousand year old!
QC: Mr Wallace, we need you to simply answer the question.
UNCLE: They chopped that tree down—
QC: The question, Mr Wallace?
UNCLE: It was a sacred tree.
QC: Your father's name, Mr Wallace?

    UNCLE *is silent.*

Mr Wallace! Was your father's name Reginald 'Reggy' Wallace, born at Maloga in 1901?
UNCLE: That's right.

QC: And is it correct that, according to government records, your father left your family home at the Cummeragunja Reserve without you, your sister or your mother when you were seven years old.
UNCLE: He showed me all the best fishing spots. The places where the really deep holes are. He showed me what signs to look out for too. When it's the best time to fish.
QC: But he left your family when you were seven?
UNCLE: He showed me how to dive for ducks. Sneak up on them underwater and grab their legs.
QC: Mr Wallace, did your father leave your family when you were seven years old?

    UNCLE *is silent.*

According to government records, your father was removed from the reserve for illegal alcohol use? Is that correct?
UNCLE: He was a top shearer. A hard worker.
QC: Mr Wallace, I will re-phrase the question. Is it correct—?
UNCLE: He was taken off.
QC: For illegal alcohol use?

    UNCLE *does not answer.*

Mr Wallace, is it correct that, according to the Aborigines Protection Board records, you were removed at the age of nine and put into child welfare?
UNCLE: Who told you that?!
QC: Please answer the question.
UNCLE: I don't want to talk about that.
QC: Mr Wallace—
UNCLE: I've come to talk about the land.
QC: Mr Wallace, were you in child welfare, and away from the reserve for over twenty years?
UNCLE: I spent the best part of my childhood running away from black cars!
QC: Were you away from the land in question for twenty years?
UNCLE: We were told to swim across the other side of the river if we saw 'em. Stick to the riverbank.
QC: Mr Wallace, the question was—

ACT TWO

UNCLE: My mother! She didn't cry for days or weeks or months. She cried for years! Looking for us.

QC: I'm sorry, Mr Wallace, we are asking you to verify whether you were put into child welfare when you were nine years of age. Yes, or no?

UNCLE: We just want our land back!

QC: And were you away from the land from the time you were nine years old and did not return until you were the age of thirty? Is that correct?

UNCLE: I've been back for fifty years.

QC: But you were away from the land for twenty years?

UNCLE: [*pointing to his heart*] Not in here.

QC: Yes, Mr Wallace. However, you did leave the area when you were nine and were you away then for over twenty years?

Silence.

UNCLE: That's it.

Pause.

QC: And your sister? I believe you have a sister?

Pause.

UNCLE: Yes.

QC: Her name?

UNCLE *is silent.*

Mr Wallace, can you please state the name of your sister for the court records?

UNCLE *is silent.*

Mr Wallace...?

UNCLE *is silent.*

Her name?

Pause.

UNCLE: She died.

Pause.

QC: Mr Wallace, we need her name. For the records.

UNCLE: Mae. Little Mae.

QC: Thank you, Mr Wallace. You may stand down.
UNCLE: I have other things to say!
QC: That's all for now. Thank you, Mr Wallace. The court will call the next witness.
UNCLE: What about the canoe tree?!

> UNCLE *stays on the stand. The lights fade.*

QC: Thank you, Mr Wallace.

♦ ♦ ♦ ♦ ♦

SCENE TWENTY: WAR PAINT

It is night time at Munarra's camp. A storm is brewing. Electricity fills the air.

Seated by a fire, the DINGOES *are sharpening their spears.* MUNARRA *is kneeling by the fire and is surrounded by broken pieces of Curr's teacup. With her digging stick she grinds the porcelain to powder. She spits on the powder and, with war on her mind, paints her face and body with the clay. They recite the words 'nyini dhan' [to fight] and 'Ngatha batima dinyuwinya' [I will spear him now].*

♦ ♦ ♦ ♦ ♦

SCENE TWENTY-ONE: THE WAY HOME

Late at night at Uncle's camp.

UNCLE *takes off his best shirt, screws it up and throws it at the base of a tree. He opens a beer and swigs. Suddenly the bell from his fishing rod goes off. He dives for it and has a monumental struggle with the fish on the end.*

UNCLE: Woo. Look out! Bloody hell! Who's knocking on me door?

> *He dashes to the line and carefully reels it.*

Ooooooh, it's a big one! Come on, big fulla, don't get away on me now!

> *He hooks the fish.*

I got him, I got him, I got him, I got him! I got the big fish! See? I got him.

The fish on the end of the line is huge. UNCLE *pulls the line in.*

Come on, old fulla. I've hooked you, ya mongrel. Come on. I've got ya. I've been after you. Come on, big fulla. I've got ya.

He hauls the fish to the surface and sits on the bank exhausted.

Jesus Christ! You're uglier than I thought you'd be. Harold bloody Withers come back to haunt me.

With one last heave he hauls the fish up onto the bank. He catches his breath.

I got you now. I got ya.

He looks into the face of the fish, gasping for air. It's as though he sees his entire life flash before his eyes.

I knew I'd catch ya. Sooner or later. Later, rather than sooner. Now I see you. All silver and green and smelly. You look to be three hundred year old. My dad said if you split open the guts of a fish you can see its entire life journey mapped out. All the creeks and rivers the fish has swum. You see it all like a tree. That's your birth tree. Where the fish was born and where it will die. That's what my dad said. I see you now, Harold. Your time is up, old fulla. So is mine.

He looks into the face of the fish once more. He hears death calling. He unhooks the fish and lets it go.

Now go on, Harold! Get away from this fishing hole. You're too old to eat now. Go on!

He throws a stick into the water, exhausted, and watches the fish float away. The wind changes its tune and MAE*'s voice leads him slowly into the darkness of the bush.*

MAE: [*whispering*] Albert! Albert!
UNCLE: Mae?

He walks further, trying to find the source of the voice.

MAE: Albert!
UNCLE: Is that you, Mae?
MAE: Where are you, Albert?

UNCLE: I'm here, Mae.

He sees the spirits of MAE *and* LITTLE ALBERT *huddled together.*

Mae.

MAE: Are we lost, Albert?

LITTLE ALBERT & UNCLE: [*together*] Yeah, I think we are, Mae.

MAE: Oooh, Albert.

UNCLE *crouches to comfort* MAE *and* LITTLE ALBERT.

UNCLE & LITTLE ALBERT: [*together*] It's okay, Mae. Remember when we went up the river that day? Up at our favourite tree. 'Grelba' we called him. Remember?

A tree illuminates, inviting him.

UNCLE: Nope. Not that one.

As UNCLE *tells the story, he looks for his tree.*

UNCLE & LITTLE ALBERT: [*together*] And we played and played and played there for hours.

UNCLE: Hanging off branches. Dangling our feet in the river, playing with the current. We played mudsticks that day, remember? [*Still looking for his tree*] Nah. Not that one… And then it got dark. Too dark and we was miiiiiles from home. We'd been told about that little Hairy Bekka, ay? We didn't know which way to go so we took off from the river, through the bush and over to the plains. And we're walking real slow and quiet so that Hairy Bekka don't catch us.

MAE *begins to cry.*

MAE: Albert, I'm scared.

LITTLE ALBERT & UNCLE: [*together*] Sshhhh, Mae, sshhhh. Hairy Bekka come get us.

MAE: That Bekka! She's real hairy. She's gonna take us away on her back and throw her tit over her shoulder to us.

LITTLE ALBERT & UNCLE: [*together*] Sshhhh, Mae!

LITTLE ALBERT *puts his hand over* MAE*'s mouth. He gently sits her on the ground and, rocking her, sings 'Inanay'. Finally,* UNCLE *comes to the base of his tree.*

UNCLE: The wind is picking up and it's getting real dark …

The min min lights shine on his face.

And then we see these lights… waaaaaayyyy off in the distance.

His mother's spirit appears.

MAE: It's Mum, it's Mum, she's put a lantern in the tree.

UNCLE: Alinta! Those lights they were swaying from side to side. We walked straight towards that light and we were so happy, 'cause we thought we weren't gonna see our mum and dad ever again! And when we got home we copped the biggest hiding! No dinner! We were starving! And…

Becoming weaker now, he sits at the base of his tree.

When it was safe to talk again, I said to Mum…

LITTLE ALBERT: Hey, Mum… we saw the lantern in the tree…

LITTLE ALBERT & MAE: [*together*] From way out there.

UNCLE: And she said, 'What lantern? What are you talking about? You're lucky that Bekka didn't catch you!' It was the min min lights that showed us the way home.

Pause.

LITTLE ALBERT & MAE: [*together*] Gukai!

UNCLE: They showed us the way home.

The lights shine brighter now. UNCLE *stares into them. He lays down and prepares for his death.*

MAE: Cummeragunja.

LITTLE ALBERT: … Home.

A curlew sounds.

♦ ♦ ♦ ♦ ♦

SCENE TWENTY-TWO: A MATTER OF SECONDS

Darkness. Thunder. The large ticking of a clock which ends abruptly. The TELLERS *enter.*

TELLER 3: Nineteen seconds.

Pause for nineteen seconds.

TELLER 2: In nineteen seconds I can open an envelope, look at its contents, know that it's junk mail and throw it out.
TELLER 1: In nineteen seconds I can turn the television on, channel surf five stations until I find the show I like.

The TELLERS *begin to overlap each other.*

TELLER 3: I can light a cigarette, put the smoke in my lungs and put it out again.
TELLER 2: I can make a telephone call and find out no-one is home.
TELLER 3: I can read and digest the *Woman's Day* from cover to cover.
TELLER 1: I can put milk in my tea and stir it.
TELLER 2: I can track down and swat three flies.
TELLER 3: I can put the cat out.
TELLER 1: In nineteen seconds I can recite a nursery rhyme.
ALL: [*together, singing*]
    Baa baa black sheep,
    Have you any wool?
    Yes sir, yes sir,
    Three bags full:
    One for the master and…

The nursery rhyme is broken by three loud knocks.

QC: All rise!

The QC *enters and mumbles the judgement incoherently.*

The court determines that native title does not exist in relation to the areas of land and waters identified to Schedule D to Native Title Determination Application FVN 94/1 accepted by the Native Title Registrar on 26 May 1994.

He bangs his hammer again and leaves.

TELLER 1: Nineteen seconds.
TELLER 2: Nineteen seconds.
TELLER 3: Nineteen seconds.
ALL: [*together*] Nineteen seconds.

♦ ♦ ♦ ♦ ♦

ACT TWO 49

SCENE TWENTY-THREE: FROZEN IN COMBAT

In dim darkness, CURR *begins to chuckle. The smug laughter of victory. Ongoing and relentless to the* TELLERS' *ears. Electricity fills the air. A storm is threatening as the land rises up in opposition. In full war regalia,* MUNARRA *and the* DINGOES *pick up their weapons.* MUNARRA *lets out a defiant war cry and the land follows suit, billowing up the storm.* CURR's *chuckling is incessant.*

The storm rages and furiously peaks. Redgums sway violently, their branches groaning precariously as MUNARRA *and the* DINGOES *approach* CURR—*his victorious laughter cutting through them like a knife. They inch forward with revenge as* CURR *stands, fumbling for his gun.* MUNARRA *screams to rid the land of this curse and lunges forward with her digging stick. At the point of contact...*

The world freezes...

An in-breath.

MUNARRA *and* CURR.

Frozen in combat.

A statue of ANZAC proportions.

Weapons raised, we see the whites of MUNARRA's *eyes.*

CURR *is petrified.*

The land is restless.

The lights fade.

✦ ✦ ✦ ✦ ✦

SCENE TWENTY-FOUR: JUDGEMENT DAY

It is late at night at Uncle's camp. The fire is almost out.
LYALL *enters, looking for* UNCLE.

LYALL: Uncle! Uncle! Are you there? [*Pause.*] Damn! Where are you?
    He checks UNCLE's *lines and sees they haven't been baited.*
Uncle?
    Realising UNCLE *is not at the camp,* LYALL *sits down by the fire and practises talking to him.*

Uncle, I came here as soon as I could. [*Pause.*] I just wanted to... Nah! [*Pause.*] Um... Uncle, they finished court today. I just wanted to let you know that... we... Shit! [*Pause.*] Uncle, they finished at the court today. Auntie Lou was there and a lot of the old ones. We loaded up the bus this morning. Brought our flag with us. I was real nervous all the way up. Couldn't even eat. 'Judgement Day': that's what Auntie Lola called it. But I called it 'A Day of Hope', ay? [*Pause.*] Uncle... we lost. 'Tide of history' they called it. [*Pause.*] I'm sorry I made you go to that court. [*Pause.*] What's gonna happen, Uncle?

He gets up and looks around one last time. He stokes the fire and leaves.

◆ ◆ ◆ ◆ ◆

SCENE TWENTY-FIVE: THANK YOU, BUT...

MUNARRA *stands alone, surrounded by a cluster of tree stumps. She holds her blood-soaked digging stick.* CURR *is seated on his chair. A foul wind blows.*

A group of MEN *appear behind* MUNARRA. *They are wearing Driza-Bones and hats and carry shovels. They each begin to dig a hole in the earth.*

MUNARRA: I see you! [*Pause.*] I can see you there! [*Pause.*] I see! Are you happy with what has become of this place?

The MEN *do not respond and continue to shovel to a beat.*

Come closer.

The shovelling stops. They look at her.

Come closer.

They do not move.

Come closer.

They begin to shovel again, maintaining their hypnotic beat.

Yes. I can smell you. I remember that smell. What happened here?

The MEN *stop for one beat. And then continue.*

What happened when time arrived at this place?

They shovel faster.

I see! You are driving us to distraction. Leading us to despair. You have taken. And now you give us death! Untimely death to relieve us from what you have made. Are you waiting for my death? Are you?

The shovelling continues.

You're digging my grave!

The MEN *shovel even faster.*

You may dig my grave! [*Pause.*] But as long as this river flows, the lake fills and floods, the redgums sway and grow—we are here. For as long as the eagle flies and the long-neck turtle swims—we are here. Like every grain of sand on our river's shores—we are here. Like the line that connects me to my traditions—we are here. Like every leaf on every branch on every tree on this land—we are here. We are here! We are here!

The MEN *stop shovelling and fade out of existence. They shed their Driza-Bones and join* MUNARRA *in a line of defiance. A war stance.*

And I am not your judgement.
I am not your 'Exhibit A'.
I am not your servant.
I am Yorta Yorta.
We are Yorta Yorta.
And…
WE… ARE… HERE.

They close their eyes. A reflection of the opening of the play—remembering and acknowledging Yorta Yorta land and people. A montage of images fills the space, emerging out of the land and onto the TELLERS. *Yorta Yorta people past and present. The next generation. The sound of a group of elders singing the song 'Bura Fera' echoes out in celebration of the endurance of Yorta Yorta survival and spirit.*

Finally, one last image remains. It states:

> *This is an important*
> *ABORIGINAL SITE.*
> *It is an offence to*

> *enter, deface, damage or*
> *otherwise interfere with*
> *this site.*
>
> *Penalty:*
> *1. Up to $10,000 or 5 years jail or both.*
> *2. If the person is a body corporate, $50,000.*
>
> *Signed:*
> CNR Area Manager   Yorta Yorta Clans Group

Fade to black.

THE END

www.currency.com.au

Visit Currency Press' website now to:

- Buy your books online
- Browse through our full list of titles, from plays to screenplays, books on theatre, film and music, and more
- Choose a play for your school or amateur performance group by cast size and gender
- Obtain information about performance rights
- Find out about theatre productions and other performing arts news across Australia
- For students, read our study guides
- For teachers, access syllabus and other relevant information
- Sign up for our email newsletter

The performing arts publisher